A SON WHO RAN AWAY

by Kyle Butt

Illustrated by Ken Perkins

A Son Who Ran Away
by Kyle Butt

ISBN -10: 1-60063-000-6
ISBN-13: 978-1-60063-000-2
Library of Congress: 2007921931

Cover and Artwork by Ken Perkins

Printed in China

Apologetics Press, Inc.
230 Landmark Drive
Montgomery, Alabama 36117
U.S.A.

Jesus told a story
Of a man who had two sons.

The older boy stayed home
But not the younger one.

The younger son decided
That he would leave his dad,

Taking lots of money
And everything he had.

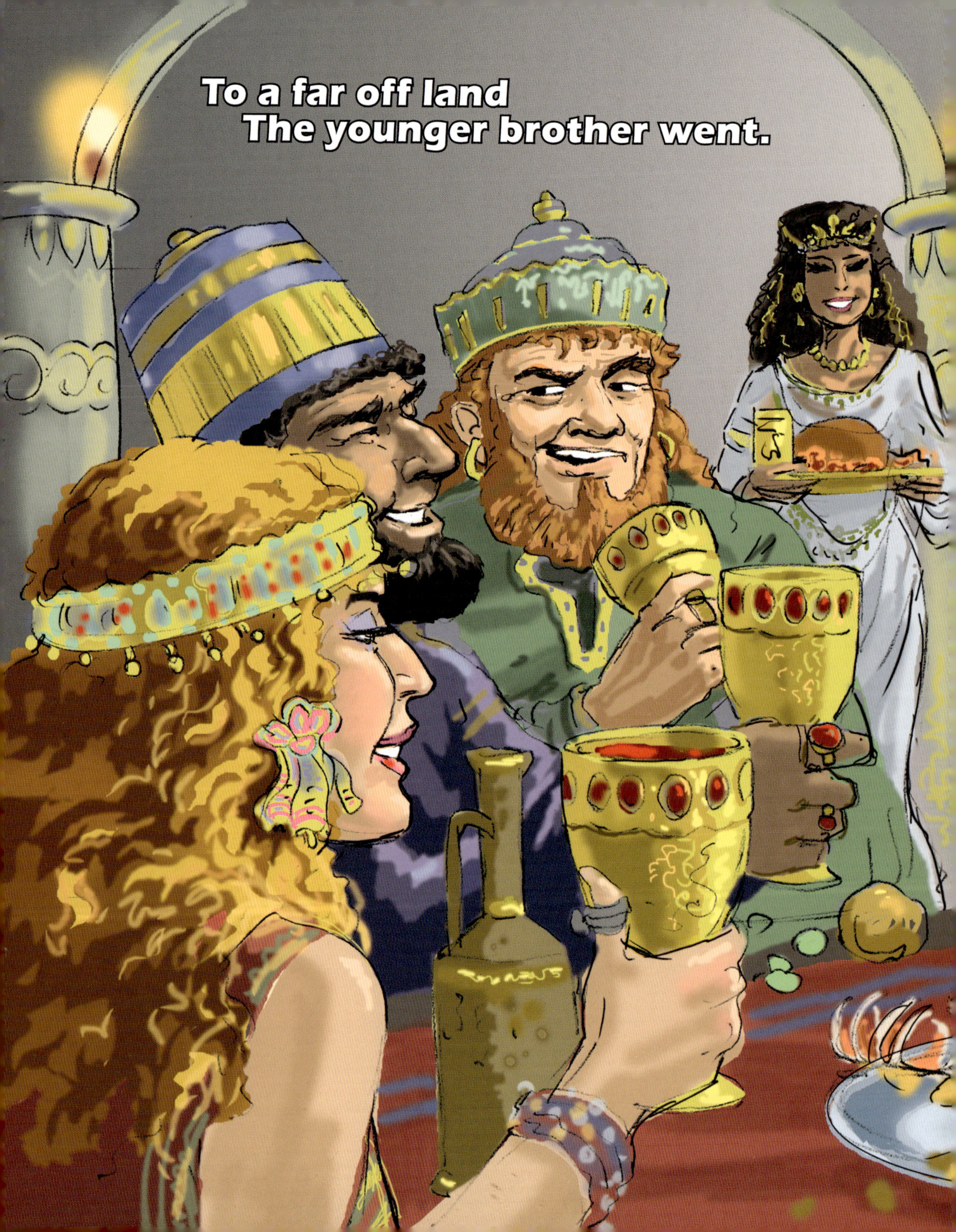

To a far off land
The younger brother went.

Where he wasted all his money
Every bit of it was spent.

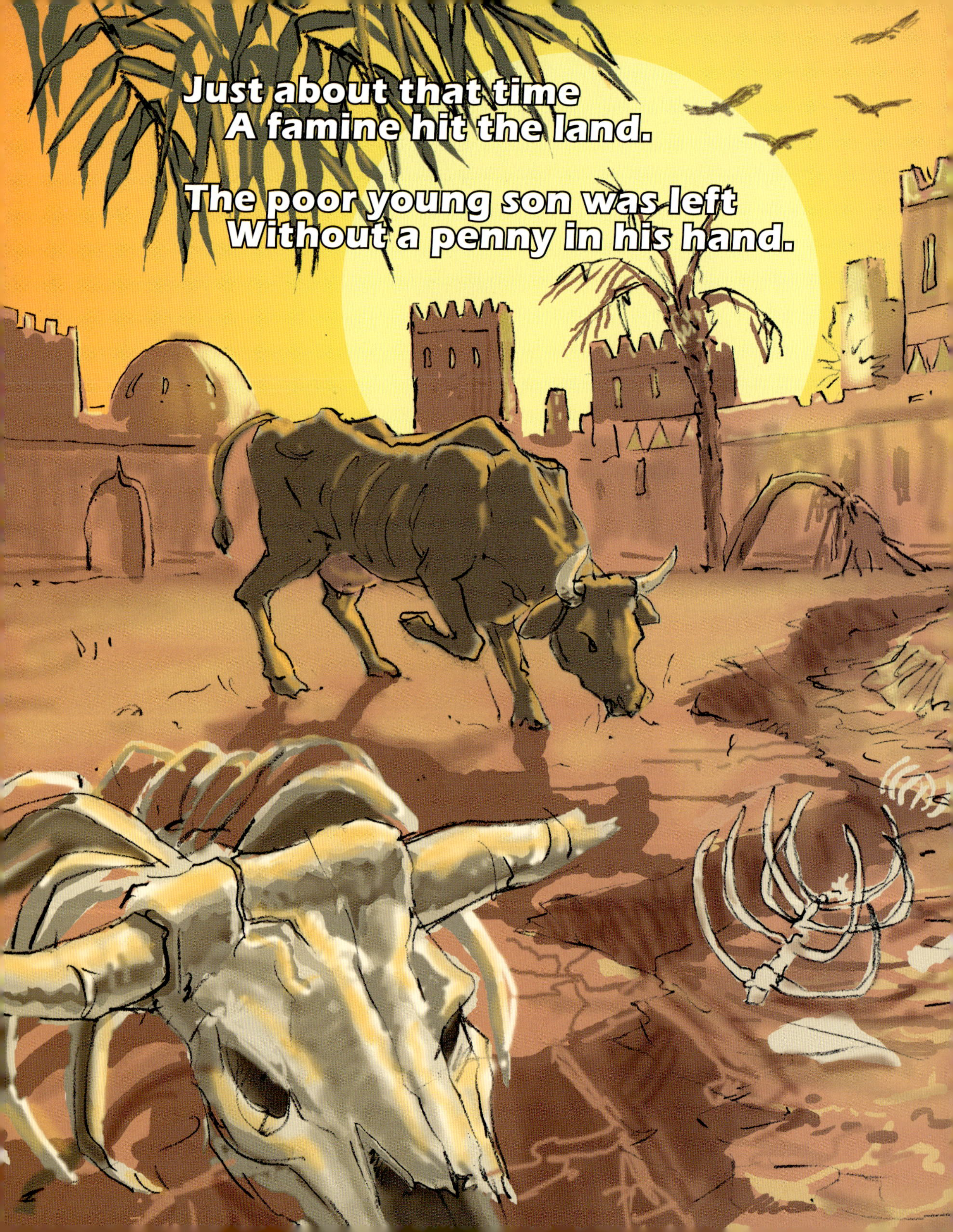

Just about that time
A famine hit the land.

The poor young son was left
Without a penny in his hand.

He started getting hungry
But his money was all gone.

What ever would he do
In this strange land all alone?

He took a job feeding pigs
But the famine kept on going.

Even pig slop started looking good
As his hunger kept on growing.

Then the son decided
He had been very wrong,

To leave his loving family
And stay away so long.

He wanted to go home
To confess his awful sin.

Maybe his loving father
Would take him back again.

All the long way home
He considered what to say.

But his father spotted him
While he was far away.

His father ran to him,
He hugged him and he kissed him.

The younger son could tell
That he had really missed him.

The father loved the son
And forgave him of his sins.

He was very happy
To have him home again.

Then they held a feast
In honor of the boy.

The father and his son
Were filled with lots of joy.

And so it is with God
If His children run away,

He will always take them back
When they're sorry and obey.

Just like the caring father,
God has loved us all along.

And it hurts Him very much
Whenever we do wrong.

But when we stop our sin
And start doing what is right,

God runs out to greet us
Any day or any night.

So if you ever wonder
If God loves you when you stray,

Just remember the young son
Who came back home to stay.